EXPLORING COUNTRIES

Finland

by Megan Borgert-Spaniol

BELLWETHER MEDIA • MINNEAPOLIS, MN

Note to Librarians, Teachers, and Parents:

Blastoff! Readers are carefully developed by literacy experts and combine standards-based content with developmentally appropriate text.

Level 1 provides the most support through repetition of high-frequency words, light text, predictable sentence patterns, and strong visual support.

Level 2 offers early readers a bit more challenge through varied simple sentences, increased text load, and less repetition of high-frequency words.

Level 3 advances early-fluent readers toward fluency through increased text and concept load, less reliance on visuals, longer sentences, and more literary language.

Level 4 builds reading stamina by providing more text per page, increased use of punctuation, greater variation in sentence patterns, and increasingly challenging vocabulary.

Level 5 encourages children to move from "learning to read" to "reading to learn" by providing even more text, varied writing styles, and less familiar topics.

Whichever book is right for your reader, Blastoff! Readers are the perfect books to build confidence and encourage a love of reading that will last a lifetime!

This edition first published in 2014 by Bellwether Media, Inc.

No part of this publication may be reproduced in whole or in part without written permission of the publisher. For information regarding permission, write to Bellwether Media, Inc., Attention: Permissions Department, 5357 Penn Avenue South, Minneapolis, MN 55419.

Library of Congress Cataloging-in-Publication Data

Borgert-Spaniol, Megan, 1989-
  Finland / by Megan Borgert-Spaniol.
    pages cm. – (Blastoff! Readers: Exploring Countries)
  Summary: "Developed by literacy experts for students in grades three through seven, this book introduces young readers to the geography and culture of Finland"– Provided by publisher.
  Includes bibliographical references and index.
  ISBN 978-1-62617-066-7 (hardcover : alk. paper)
  1. Finland–Juvenile literature. I. Title.
DL1012.B67 2014
948.97–dc23

2013033614

Printed in the United States of America, North Mankato, MN.

Contents

Finland is a country in northern Europe. This long, narrow land covers 130,559 square miles (338,145 square kilometers). Sweden touches Finland in the northwest. Norway is its neighbor to the north. Finland shares its long eastern border with Russia.

In the southwest, the **Gulf** of Bothnia extends north from the Baltic Sea. It runs along Finland's western coast. The Gulf of Finland washes onto the country's southern shore. The capital city of Helsinki is located here. This major **seaport** is the northernmost capital on the European **continent**.

Norway

Sweden

Russia

Gulf of
Bothnia

Finland

Helsinki

Gulf of
Finland

N

W   E

S

Baltic
Sea

Did you know?

The region inside the Arctic Circle is known as the Land of the Midnight Sun. In summer, the sun doesn't set for days at a time.

Thousands of sparkling lakes dot central and southeast Finland. Between them run forests of pine, spruce, and birch trees. To the south and west, lowlands dip into a long and ragged shoreline. Thousands of small islands rise up through the chilly waters off the coast.

In southern Finland, summers are short and winters are cold. The climate is much harsher in the northern third of the country. This hilly region falls within the **Arctic Circle**. In winter, the skies of northern Finland glow with the dancing colors of **northern lights**.

northern lights

Lake Saimaa

The Saimaa Lake District is the largest lake system in Finland. It is made up of about 120 lakes that are connected by narrow **channels**. More than 14,000 islands dot the waters. The largest lake, Lake Saimaa, is in the southeastern corner of the network.

Tourists and adventurers of all kinds flock to the Saimaa Lake District. Kayakers cut through the cool blue water past rocky, forested islands. Bicyclists pedal along shoreline paths and over bridges with breathtaking views. **Steamboats** carry passengers through the maze of water and land. Some cruise ships travel to and from Helsinki through the Saimaa **Canal** and the Gulf of Finland.

fun fact

The fun does not end when the lakes freeze over. In winter, skaters glide over icy trails that run across the frozen fields of white.

Saimaa
ringed seal

Forests cover three-quarters of Finland. Birch, maple, and other **deciduous trees** grow in the south. Pines extend through most of the country, including the far north. Finland's forests are home to such majestic animals as the brown bear, lynx, and gray wolf. Minks, weasels, and other small mammals hide nearby.

gray wolf

mink

great spotted
woodpecker

Finland provides food and shelter for more than 450
species of birds. Great spotted woodpeckers bring
flashes of red to the country's forests. In the north, great
gray owls swoop down to snatch rodents from the snow.
Whooper swans return to northern wetlands in the spring.
At the coast, **migrating** Arctic terns search for food
along the rocky shore.

Sami people

More than five million people call Finland home. About nine out of every ten of them are Finnish. Swedish people make up the next largest group. Most Swedish-speaking people live along the southern coast or on the Åland Islands to the southwest. Small populations of Russians, Estonians, Romani, and Sami also live in Finland. The Sami descend from **native** peoples who arrived in the country thousands of years ago. They live in Lapland, Finland's northernmost region.

Finnish and Swedish are the official languages of Finland. The Sami speak their own languages. Finnish people are very proud of their heritage. They use the word *sisu* to describe themselves. *Sisu* is a combination of strength, determination, and **perseverance**.

Speak Finnish!

English	Finnish	How to say it
hello	hei	hey
good-bye	näkemiin	KNACK-eh-meen
yes	kyllä	KOO-lah
no	ei	AY-ee
please	ole hyvä	OH-lay WHO-vah
thank you	kiitos	KEE-tohss
friend	ystävä	OO-stah-vah

Did you know?

Finland is known for its efforts to give women equal access to power. Many of the country's top business and government positions are held by women.

Finland's largest cities and towns are clustered along the country's southern coast. Most city-dwellers live in apartments. They take cars, buses, and trains to work. Those who live in Helsinki can get around on the city's **subway**. Several airlines fly passengers between different parts of the country. Travelers can also cross Finland's waters on **ferries**.

Finns enjoy a high quality of life. Most people stay connected with mobile phones and the Internet. Families have easy access to health care, education, and the arts. Finns also benefit from clean water and air and plenty of natural areas. Many escape to summer cottages along the country's beautiful forests, lakes, and coastal waters.

countryside 15%

cities 85%

Children in Finland begin school when they are 7 years old. They study Finnish, math, and science. They also take classes in music, arts and crafts, and sports. In third and fourth grade, students begin to learn English and Swedish. Later subjects include history, biology, and geography.

Students must attend school until they are 16 years old. After that, some choose to learn a **trade**. They are trained to work at hospitals, construction sites, and other jobs. Most students move on to three years of high school. They take classes that prepare them for higher education. Many attend the University of Helsinki, the country's largest university.

Where People Work
in Finland

manufacturing 15.5%

farming 4.4%

services 80.1%

Most Finns have **service jobs**. These people work in government offices, banks, and other businesses. They also serve the country's tourists at restaurants, hotels, and shops. Many workers have jobs in **manufacturing**. They produce machinery and electronics that are sold to other countries. Craftspeople make world-famous glassware, pottery, and furniture.

Finland's most important **natural resource** is wood. Lumber is hauled from the forests and sent floating down rivers. It ends up at factories that produce paper and wood products. Farmers in the south and west grow grains, potatoes, and sugar beets. They also raise cattle, chickens, and pigs. A few Sami still herd reindeer in the north.

pesäpallo

Spending time outdoors is a way of life in Finland. During the summer, families gather to swim, canoe, and play games at lakeside cabins. Some go sailing through the Åland Islands off the coast. In cities, people fill stadiums to watch *pesäpallo* matches. This Finnish sport is similar to American baseball.

Winter in Finland brings ice skating, snowshoeing, and cross-country skiing. Brave swimmers feel refreshed after a dip in icy lake waters. Young Finns like to play and watch ice hockey. They cheer for the national team as it battles Sweden and other countries. When they are not outside, Finns enjoy browsing through local libraries. Evenings are spent at movies, concerts, and theater performances.

fun fact

Several goofy sports were invented in Finland. The country hosts annual world championships in wife carrying, mobile phone throwing, and swamp football.

swamp football

Did you know?

Restaurant Day was born in Helsinki in 2011. Four times a year, anyone can sell homemade dishes from parks, street corners, and doorsteps for a full day.

For many Finns, food has a strong connection to nature. Those who visit summer cottages grill vegetables, sausages, and fish in the open air. Some uncover mushrooms and pluck berries from forests. The plump orange cloudberry is a national delight found in Finland's northern swamps. Finns pair this tart fruit with cheese or cook it into jam.

Hearty meals fill the Finnish winter. Reindeer stew is a **traditional** meal served with mashed potatoes and lingonberry sauce. Karelian pie is another favorite. Its rye crust and rice filling are eaten with a special egg butter. A common side dish is boiled potatoes tossed in butter and fresh dill. Good meals end with coffee and a sweet, spiced bread called *pulla*.

cloudberries

Karelian pie

Easter

24

Most Finns celebrate Christmas and Easter. On Christmas Eve, families light candles at the graves of loved ones. Later they feast on ham, salmon, herring, and other seasonal dishes. Around Easter, children dress up as witches and deliver willow branches to their neighbors. They receive candy or coins in return.

May Day, or *Vappu*, is a popular springtime holiday. University students wear their school hats to parties and picnics. Everyone sips *sima*, a bubbly lemon drink. They also snack on sugary fried cakes called *tippaleipä*. Midsummer is a festival in late June that celebrates the warm season. Finns light great bonfires and dance into the bright night.

For most Finns, the **sauna** is a weekly practice. Traditional saunas are small wooden huts. Inside, burning wood is used to heat stones. Finns sit or lie down on raised benches along the walls. They pour water on the hot stones to create steam. Saunas often reach temperatures greater than 200 degrees Fahrenheit (93 degrees Celsius).

! fun fact
Finns bring bundles of leafy birch twigs into the sauna. They lightly whip themselves with the twigs to massage their muscles and cleanse their skin.

Saunas can be found in Finland's homes, apartments, and office buildings. People even attach them to cars, buses, and boats. The most natural setting for a sauna is the lakeside cabin. After sweating in the hot steam, Finns dive into the cool water. In winter, they often jump into a pile of snow. This relaxing **ritual** is thought to heal the body and mind. It offers the same peace and quiet that Finns seek in their country's natural beauty.

Fast Facts About Finland

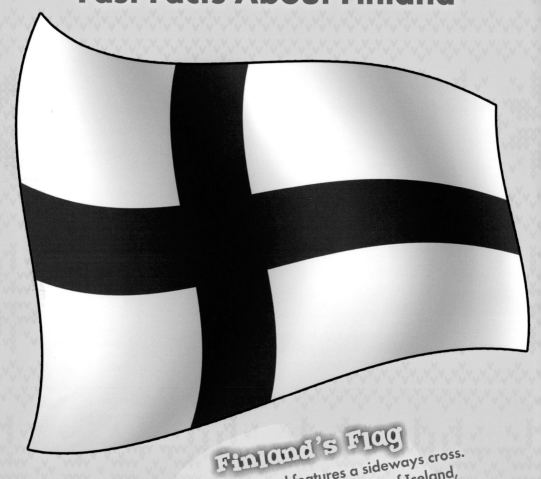

Finland's Flag

The flag of Finland features a sideways cross. This same design is on the flags of Iceland, Denmark, Norway, and Sweden. They are known as the Nordic flags. The blue color of Finland's cross represents the country's lakes. The white background honors its snow. This flag was adopted on May 29, 1918.

Official Name: Republic of Finland

Area: 130,559 square miles (338,145 square kilometers); Finland is the 65th largest country in the world.

Capital City:	Helsinki
Important Cities:	Espoo, Tampere, Oulu, Turku
Population:	5,266,114 (July 2013)
Official Languages:	Finnish, Swedish
National Holiday:	Independence Day (December 6)
Religions:	Christian (84.7%), none (15.1%), other (0.2%)
Major Industries:	services, manufacturing, forestry
Natural Resources:	lumber, water, copper, nickel, zinc
Manufactured Products:	electronics, machinery, wood products, paper products
Farm Products:	grains, potatoes, sugar beets, milk, beef, poultry, pork
Unit of Money:	Euro; the euro is divided into 100 cents.

Glossary

Arctic Circle—the northernmost region in the world

canal—a waterway that is built to connect larger bodies of water

channels—natural waterways that connect bodies of water

continent—one of the seven main land areas on Earth; the continents are Africa, Antarctica, Asia, Australia, Europe, North America, and South America.

deciduous trees—trees that lose their leaves every year

ferries—boats that carry passengers across bodies of water

gulf—part of an ocean or sea that extends into land

hearty—filling and satisfying

manufacturing—a field of work in which people use machines to make products

migrating—traveling from one place to another, often with the seasons

native—originally from a specific place

natural resource—a material that is taken from the earth and used to make products or fuel

northern lights—colorful natural lights that appear in the sky; northern lights most commonly occur within or near the Arctic Circle.

perseverance—the ability to work through difficulties without giving up

ritual—a regular practice that is considered sacred or spiritual

sauna—a dry heat bath or steam bath, or the room in which such a bath is taken

seaport—a coastal city or town where ships can dock

service jobs—jobs that perform tasks for people or businesses

steamboats—boats powered by steam

subway—an underground train system

tourists—people who travel to visit another place

trade—a job or craft that requires learned skill

traditional—relating to a custom, idea, or belief handed down from one generation to the next

To Learn More

AT THE LIBRARY

Alatalo, Jaakko. *Iina-Marja's Day: From Dawn to Dusk in Lapland*. London, U.K.: Frances Lincoln Children's Books, 2011.

Bianco, Margery, and James Cloyd Bowman. *Tales From a Finnish Tupa*. Minneapolis, Minn.: University of Minnesota Press, 2009.

Clark, Geri. *Finland*. New York, N.Y.: Children's Press, 2009.

ON THE WEB

Learning more about Finland is as easy as 1, 2, 3.

1. Go to www.factsurfer.com.

2. Enter "Finland" into the search box.

3. Click the "Surf" button and you will see a list of related Web sites.

With factsurfer.com, finding more information is just a click away.

Index